BEFORE YOU START!

You are exactly where you are meant to be right now, on the path to achieving your biggest goals ~ you haven't stumbled upon this journal by accident! And through aligning with your higher self by taking consistent action towards these goals, you will be rewarded in huge ways.

So here is your first reward.. A FREE guided alignment meditation that you can listen to anytime you feel you're falling off track. It's less than 10 minutes long which is perfect for a quick re-alignment whenever you need it.

This is your first gift from the universe of many. Abundance is coming to you!

Just send the word 'alignment' to @TheMagicWithin_ on Instagram to receive your gift.

It's time to make some serious progress!

"*A goal without a plan is just a wish.*"
~ Antoine de Saint-Exupéry

There is a life you fantasize about, big goals you dream of achieving, and a reality that is filled with abundance and your deepest desires. And the truth is, **you can have it all**. But you must align with the version of yourself who is in that dream life.

By achieving small goals each week and regularly reflecting, you will make consistent changes, mind, body and soul - gradually aligning with the highest version of yourself - the version who has it all.

THEMAGICWITHIN

During this alignment process, you will actually be changing yourself on an energetic and physical level, which is why this journal doesn't just focus on one area of goal setting. Each week you'll find a space to set some main goals, as well as a space to plan something for your body, your mind and your soul. It is the alignment and enhancement of all of these things, and the balance between them, that will bring you all you desire.

Each week you will also find a reminder of how capable you are of achieving your goals, as well as the chance to write how grateful you are for all you have along your journey. Gratitude attracts abundance and with the combination of action taking and cultivating an abundance mindset, using this journal regularly means it is only a matter of time until you are living in your dream life as your higher self.

This life is too short to keep dreaming about who you want to be, it's time to become that person!

THEMAGICWITHIN

YOUR PLEDGE TO YOURSELF..

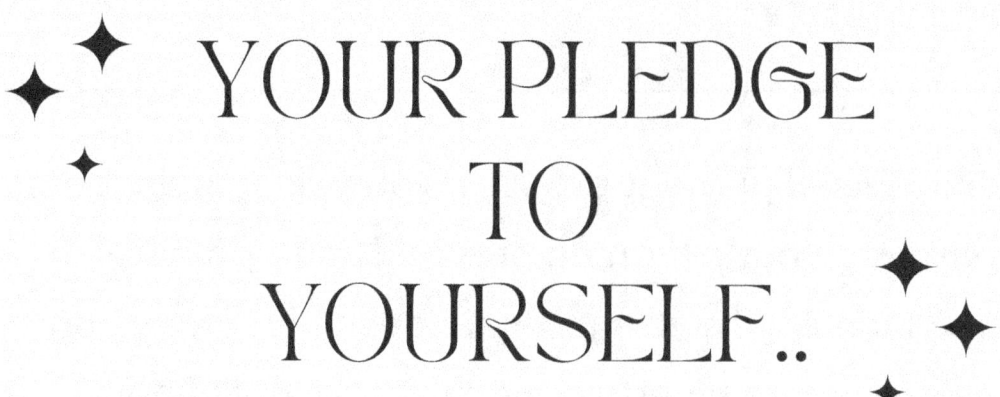

As all you need to live a magical life is already within you, you just need to make the effort to explore yourself more and commit to achieving your goals - if you do that you will be living the life of your dreams before you know it. So this is your chance to make a promise to yourself that you can look back on anytime you feel like giving up - no matter how tough external circumstances may get, or may already be, no matter how tired you may feel, stick to this pledge that you won't give up on yourself. YOU are the one experiencing this miracle that is life, you are meant to enjoy it!

Commitment and alignment will have you experiencing your wildest dreams in no time.

I _____ promise myself that I will stay committed to discovering my inner magic by self reflecting and achieving my goals weekly. I know that if I do this, huge rewards will enter my life and I will be able to view the world in a different way.

I have all I need to live my happiest life, I just need to stay dedicated to the journey.

Sign here: .... Date: ....

THEMAGICWITHIN

Week 1

DATE _____

MY MAIN GOALS FOR THE UPCOMING WEEK ARE:

○ _____

○ _____

○ _____

It's a Bonus if I...

_____

_____

I Will Move My Body By:

_____

_____

I Will Enhance My Mind By:

_____

_____

I Will Please My Soul By:

_____

_____

REMINDER:

The past does not define you. Each moment is a fresh start. Let go of the past and use this next week to cultivate all you desire - because you can truly receive all you're wishing for.

I AM GOING INTO THIS WEEK FEELING...

_____

AFFIRM:

I am deserving of all I desire. I can and will have all I'm striving for, it's just a matter of time.

Week 1 Check In

DATE _____

THIS PAST WEEK I ACHIEVED:

- ○ _____
- ○ _____
- ○ _____
- ○ _____
- ○ _____

THIS WEEK I FELT

I AM LEAVING THIS WEEK FEELING...
_____

I Moved My Body By:

_____

_____

I Enhanced My Mind By:

_____

_____

NOTES:
_____

I Pleased My Soul By:

_____

_____

Weekly Gratitude

Date: _____

3 things I'm grateful for this week are...

_____
_____
_____

Next week I will express my gratitude by...

_____
_____
_____

"Happiness is a habit."

DATE _____

MY MAIN GOALS FOR THE UPCOMING WEEK ARE:

○ _____
○ _____
○ _____

It's a Bonus if I...

_____
_____

I Will Move My Body By:

_____
_____

I Will Enhance My Mind By:

_____
_____

I Will Please My Soul By:

_____
_____

REMINDER:
_____

You are more capable than you realise. You can literally achieve anything you put your mind to. You are going to crush this week!

I AM GOING INTO THIS WEEK FEELING...
_____

AFFIRM:
_____

I am capable of living my dream life. I already have all I need within me.

Week 2 Check In

DATE _____

THIS PAST WEEK I ACHIEVED:

- _____
- _____
- _____
- _____
- _____

I Moved My Body By:

_____
_____

I Enhanced My Mind By:

_____
_____

I Pleased My Soul By:

_____
_____

THIS WEEK I FELT

I AM LEAVING THIS WEEK FEELING...

_____

NOTES:

_____

Weekly Gratitude

Date: _____

3 things I'm grateful for this week are...

_____

_____

_____

Next week I will express my gratitude by...

_____

_____

_____

"Happiness is a habit."

DATE _____

MY MAIN GOALS FOR THE UPCOMING WEEK ARE:

○ _____

○ _____

○ _____

It's a Bonus if I...

_____

_____

I Will Move My Body By:

_____

_____

I Will Enhance My Mind By:

_____

_____

I Will Please My Soul By:

_____

_____

REMINDER:

'You are only limited by weakness of attention and poverty of imagination'
~ Neville Goddard

I AM GOING INTO THIS WEEK FEELING...

AFFIRM:

I am strong willed and determined to reach my dream life.

Week 3 Check In

DATE _____

THIS PAST WEEK I ACHIEVED:

- ○ _____
- ○ _____
- ○ _____
- ○ _____
- ○ _____

I Moved My Body By:

_____

_____

I Enhanced My Mind By:

_____

_____

I Pleased My Soul By:

_____

_____

THIS WEEK I FELT

I AM LEAVING THIS WEEK FEELING...

_____

NOTES:

_____

Weekly Gratitude

Date: _____

3 things I'm grateful for this week are...

_____

_____

_____

Next week I will express my gratitude by...

_____

_____

_____

"Happiness is a habit."

DATE _____

MY MAIN GOALS FOR THE UPCOMING WEEK ARE:

○ _____

○ _____

○ _____

It's a Bonus if I...

_____

_____

I Will Move My Body By:

_____

_____

I Will Enhance My Mind By:

_____

_____

I Will Please My Soul By:

_____

_____

REMINDER:

You have overcome 100% of your worst days. You can overcome anything this week throws at you.. with ease!

I AM GOING INTO THIS WEEK FEELING...

AFFIRM:

I am magic. I can create whatever reality I desire. And I am creating it right now.

Week 4 Check In

DATE _____

THIS PAST WEEK I ACHIEVED:

○ _____
○ _____
○ _____
○ _____
○ _____

THIS WEEK I FELT

I AM LEAVING THIS WEEK FEELING...
_____

I Moved My Body By:
_____
_____

I Enhanced My Mind By:
_____
_____

I Pleased My Soul By:
_____
_____

NOTES:
_____

Weekly Gratitude

Date: _____

3 things I'm grateful for this week are...

_____

_____

_____

Next week I will express my gratitude by...

_____

_____

_____

"Happiness is a habit."

DATE _____

MY MAIN GOALS FOR THE UPCOMING WEEK ARE:

○ _____
○ _____
○ _____

It's a Bonus if I...

_____
_____

I Will Move My Body By:

_____
_____

I Will Enhance My Mind By:

_____
_____

I Will Please My Soul By:

_____
_____

REMINDER:

There are people out there living your dream life. They are proof it is possible. There is literally no reason at all that you can't live it too. You are on your way!

I AM GOING INTO THIS WEEK FEELING...

AFFIRM:

All I desire is coming to me now. My dream life awaits me and I know I'll be living it in no time.

Week 5 Check In

DATE _____

THIS PAST WEEK I ACHIEVED:

- ○ _____
- ○ _____
- ○ _____
- ○ _____
- ○ _____

THIS WEEK I FELT

I AM LEAVING THIS WEEK FEELING...
_____

I Moved My Body By:
_____
_____

I Enhanced My Mind By:
_____
_____

NOTES:
_____

I Pleased My Soul By:
_____
_____

Weekly Gratitude

Date: _____

3 things I'm grateful for this week are...

_____
_____
_____

Next week I will express my gratitude by...

_____
_____
_____

"Happiness is a habit."

Week 6

DATE _____

MY MAIN GOALS FOR THE UPCOMING WEEK ARE:

○ _____

○ _____

○ _____

It's a Bonus if I...

_____

_____

I Will Move My Body By:

_____

_____

I Will Enhance My Mind By:

_____

_____

I Will Please My Soul By:

_____

_____

REMINDER:

Your dreams can and will all be achieved. You are working hard every week and you will get to where you want to be. Keep going.

I AM GOING INTO THIS WEEK FEELING...

AFFIRM:

I am worthy of living a life of abundance and riches.

Week 6 Check In

DATE _____

THIS PAST WEEK I ACHIEVED:

- ○ _____
- ○ _____
- ○ _____
- ○ _____
- ○ _____

I Moved My Body By:

_____

_____

I Enhanced My Mind By:

_____

_____

I Pleased My Soul By:

_____

_____

THIS WEEK I FELT

I AM LEAVING THIS WEEK FEELING...

_____

NOTES:

_____

Weekly Gratitude

Date: _____

3 things I'm grateful for this week are...

_____

_____

_____

Next week I will express my gratitude by...

_____

_____

_____

"Happiness is a habit."

Week 1

DATE _____

MY MAIN GOALS FOR THE UPCOMING WEEK ARE:

○ _____
○ _____
○ _____

It's a Bonus if I...
_____
_____

I Will Move My Body By:
_____
_____

I Will Enhance My Mind By:
_____
_____

I Will Please My Soul By:
_____
_____

REMINDER:

You are more talented than you give yourself credit for. You may have been conditioned to believe otherwise, but you have talent, you just need to keep trusting that you do.

I AM GOING INTO THIS WEEK FEELING...
_____

AFFIRM:
I am intelligent, talented and driven. This will take me places.

Week 1 Check In

DATE _____

THIS PAST WEEK I ACHIEVED:

- ○ _____
- ○ _____
- ○ _____
- ○ _____
- ○ _____

THIS WEEK I FELT

I AM LEAVING THIS WEEK FEELING...
_____

I Moved My Body By:

_____

_____

I Enhanced My Mind By:

_____

_____

NOTES:
_____

I Pleased My Soul By:

_____

_____

Weekly Gratitude

Date: _____

3 things I'm grateful for this week are...

_____

_____

_____

Next week I will express my gratitude by...

_____

_____

_____

"Happiness is a habit."

DATE _____

MY MAIN GOALS FOR THE UPCOMING WEEK ARE:

○ _____

○ _____

○ _____

It's a Bonus if I...

_____

_____

I Will Move My Body By:

_____

_____

I Will Enhance My Mind By:

_____

_____

I Will Please My Soul By:

_____

_____

REMINDER:

You are making great progress. It may seem slow, but you are well on your way to where you want to be. You just have to keep going. You've got this.

I AM GOING INTO THIS WEEK FEELING...

AFFIRM:

I am abundant and blessed. All I desire already exists and I can have it all. I will have it all.

Week 8 Check In

DATE _____

THIS PAST WEEK I ACHIEVED:

- ○ _____
- ○ _____
- ○ _____
- ○ _____
- ○ _____

I Moved My Body By:

_____

_____

I Enhanced My Mind By:

_____

_____

I Pleased My Soul By:

_____

_____

THIS WEEK I FELT

I AM LEAVING THIS WEEK FEELING...

_____

NOTES:

_____

Weekly Gratitude

Date: _____

3 things I'm grateful for this week are...

_____

_____

_____

Next week I will express my gratitude by...

_____

_____

_____

"Happiness is a habit."

Week 9

DATE _____

MY MAIN GOALS FOR THE UPCOMING WEEK ARE:

○ _____

○ _____

○ _____

It's a Bonus if I...

_____

I Will Move My Body By:

_____

_____

I Will Enhance My Mind By:

_____

_____

I Will Please My Soul By:

_____

REMINDER:

You can create your own happiness. Your life can look however you want it to look. You are designing it as you read this, you are shaping your future right now and it is looking very bright!

I AM GOING INTO THIS WEEK FEELING...

AFFIRM:

I am deserving of true happiness and the most genuine love.

Week 9 Check In

DATE _____

THIS PAST WEEK I ACHIEVED:

○ _____

○ _____

○ _____

○ _____

○ _____

THIS WEEK I FELT

I AM LEAVING THIS WEEK FEELING...
_____

I Moved My Body By:

_____

_____

I Enhanced My Mind By:

_____

_____

NOTES:
_____

I Pleased My Soul By:

_____

_____

Weekly Gratitude

Date: _____

3 things I'm grateful for this week are...

_____

_____

_____

Next week I will express my gratitude by...

_____

_____

_____

"Happiness is a habit."

Week 10

DATE _____

MY MAIN GOALS FOR THE UPCOMING WEEK ARE:

○ _____
○ _____
○ _____

It's a Bonus if I...
_____
_____

I Will Move My Body By:
_____
_____

I Will Enhance My Mind By:
_____
_____

I Will Please My Soul By:
_____
_____

REMINDER:

You are incredible just by being you. Look at you, not giving up, staying consistent.. You are making yourself proud.

I AM GOING INTO THIS WEEK FEELING...
_____

AFFIRM:
I am beautiful, inside and out.

Week 10 Check In

DATE _____

THIS PAST WEEK I ACHIEVED:

- ○ _____
- ○ _____
- ○ _____
- ○ _____
- ○ _____

I Moved My Body By:

_____
_____

I Enhanced My Mind By:

_____
_____

I Pleased My Soul By:

_____
_____

THIS WEEK I FELT

I AM LEAVING THIS WEEK FEELING...

_____

NOTES:

_____

Weekly Gratitude

Date: _____

3 things I'm grateful for this week are...

_____

_____

_____

Next week I will express my gratitude by...

_____

_____

_____

"Happiness is a habit."

Week 11

DATE _____

MY MAIN GOALS FOR THE UPCOMING WEEK ARE:

○ _____

○ _____

○ _____

It's a Bonus if I...

_____

_____

I Will Move My Body By:

_____

_____

I Will Enhance My Mind By:

_____

_____

I Will Please My Soul By:

_____

_____

REMINDER:

Your challenges are actually opportunities to learn and grow. Don't let them stop you.

I AM GOING INTO THIS WEEK FEELING...

AFFIRM:

I am unique and special just the way I am. I am magical.

Week 11 Check In

DATE _____

THIS PAST WEEK I ACHIEVED:

- ○ _____
- ○ _____
- ○ _____
- ○ _____
- ○ _____

THIS WEEK I FELT

I AM LEAVING THIS WEEK FEELING...
_____

I Moved My Body By:
_____
_____

I Enhanced My Mind By:
_____
_____

NOTES:
_____

I Pleased My Soul By:
_____
_____

Weekly Gratitude

Date: _____

3 things I'm grateful for this week are...

_____
_____
_____

Next week I will express my gratitude by...

_____
_____
_____

"Happiness is a habit."

DATE _____

MY MAIN GOALS FOR THE UPCOMING WEEK ARE:

○ _____

○ _____

○ _____

It's a Bonus if I...

_____

_____

I Will Move My Body By:

_____

_____

I Will Enhance My Mind By:

_____

_____

I Will Please My Soul By:

_____

_____

REMINDER:

You are making serious progress now. Your consistency will pay off if you keep going. Don't give up on yourself, your dream life is so close.

I AM GOING INTO THIS WEEK FEELING...

AFFIRM:

My potential has no limit. I can have all I desire, with ease.

Week 12 Check in

DATE _____

THIS PAST WEEK I ACHIEVED:

- _____
- _____
- _____
- _____
- _____

I Moved My Body By:

_____

_____

I Enhanced My Mind By:

_____

_____

I Pleased My Soul By:

_____

_____

THIS WEEK I FELT

I AM LEAVING THIS WEEK FEELING...

NOTES:

_____

Weekly Gratitude

Date: _____

3 things I'm grateful for this week are...

_____

_____

_____

Next week I will express my gratitude by...

_____

_____

_____

"Happiness is a habit."

Week 13

DATE _____

MY MAIN GOALS FOR THE UPCOMING WEEK ARE:

○ _____

○ _____

○ _____

It's a Bonus if I...

_____

_____

I Will Move My Body By:

_____

_____

I Will Enhance My Mind By:

_____

_____

I Will Please My Soul By:

_____

_____

REMINDER:

You are attracting so much abundance by continuing to work on yourself and your life. There is so much good in store for you. You will receive it all if you keep going.

I AM GOING INTO THIS WEEK FEELING...

_____

AFFIRM:

I create my own happiness.

Week 13 Check in

DATE _____

THIS PAST WEEK I ACHIEVED:

- ○ _____
- ○ _____
- ○ _____
- ○ _____
- ○ _____

I Moved My Body By:

_____

_____

I Enhanced My Mind By:

_____

_____

I Pleased My Soul By:

_____

_____

THIS WEEK I FELT

I AM LEAVING THIS WEEK FEELING...

NOTES:

Weekly Gratitude

Date: _____

3 things I'm grateful for this week are...

_____

_____

_____

Next week I will express my gratitude by...

_____

_____

_____

"Happiness is a habit."

Week 14

DATE _____

MY MAIN GOALS FOR THE UPCOMING WEEK ARE:

○ _____

○ _____

○ _____

It's a Bonus if I...

_____

_____

I Will Move My Body By:

_____

_____

I Will Enhance My Mind By:

_____

_____

I Will Please My Soul By:

_____

_____

REMINDER:

You are so capable of achieving your goals this week. You can push past tiredness, you can overcome obstacles, you can do anything you set your mind to.

I AM GOING INTO THIS WEEK FEELING...
_____

AFFIRM:

I am successful and powerful.

Week 14 Check in

DATE _____

THIS PAST WEEK I ACHIEVED:

- ○ _____
- ○ _____
- ○ _____
- ○ _____
- ○ _____

I Moved My Body By:

_____

_____

I Enhanced My Mind By:

_____

_____

I Pleased My Soul By:

_____

_____

THIS WEEK I FELT

I AM LEAVING THIS WEEK FEELING...

NOTES:

_____

Weekly Gratitude

Date: _____

3 things I'm grateful for this week are...

_____

_____

_____

Next week I will express my gratitude by...

_____

_____

_____

"Happiness is a habit."

Week 15

DATE _____

MY MAIN GOALS FOR THE UPCOMING WEEK ARE:

○ _____

○ _____

○ _____

It's a Bonus if I...

_____

_____

I Will Move My Body By:

_____

_____

I Will Enhance My Mind By:

_____

_____

I Will Please My Soul By:

_____

_____

REMINDER:

You should feel so proud that you aren't giving up on yourself and your dreams. All of the effort will be so worth it.

I AM GOING INTO THIS WEEK FEELING...

AFFIRM:

I will never, ever give up on myself.

Week 15 Check in

DATE _____

THIS PAST WEEK I ACHIEVED:

- ○ _____
- ○ _____
- ○ _____
- ○ _____
- ○ _____

THIS WEEK I FELT

I AM LEAVING THIS WEEK FEELING...
_____

I Moved My Body By:

_____

_____

I Enhanced My Mind By:

_____

_____

I Pleased My Soul By:

_____

_____

NOTES:
_____

Weekly Gratitude

Date: _____

3 things I'm grateful for this week are...

_____

_____

_____

Next week I will express my gratitude by...

_____

_____

_____

"Happiness is a habit."

Week 16

DATE _____

MY MAIN GOALS FOR THE UPCOMING WEEK ARE:

○ _____
○ _____
○ _____

It's a Bonus if I...

_____
_____

I Will Move My Body By:

_____
_____

I Will Enhance My Mind By:

_____
_____

I Will Please My Soul By:

_____
_____

REMINDER:

You are aligning with your higher self more and more each week. By staying consistent you are getting so close to living your dream life.

I AM GOING INTO THIS WEEK FEELING...

AFFIRM:

I am enough. I am complete.

Week 16 Check in

DATE _____

THIS PAST WEEK I ACHIEVED:

- ○ _____
- ○ _____
- ○ _____
- ○ _____
- ○ _____

THIS WEEK I FELT

I AM LEAVING THIS WEEK FEELING...
_____

I Moved My Body By:
_____
_____

I Enhanced My Mind By:
_____
_____

NOTES:
_____

I Pleased My Soul By:
_____
_____

Weekly Gratitude

Date: _____

3 things I'm grateful for this week are...

_____
_____
_____

Next week I will express my gratitude by...

_____
_____
_____

"Happiness is a habit."

Week 17

DATE _____

MY MAIN GOALS FOR THE UPCOMING WEEK ARE:

- ○ _____
- ○ _____
- ○ _____

REMINDER:

There truly are no limits to what you can achieve. This week will be a great one!

It's a Bonus if I...

_____
_____

I Will Move My Body By:

_____
_____

I AM GOING INTO THIS WEEK FEELING...

I Will Enhance My Mind By:

_____
_____

I Will Please My Soul By:

_____
_____

AFFIRM:

I know that whatever ability I lack, I can improve upon quickly and with ease.

Week 17 Check in

DATE _____

THIS PAST WEEK I ACHIEVED:

- ○ _____
- ○ _____
- ○ _____
- ○ _____
- ○ _____

I Moved My Body By:

_____

_____

I Enhanced My Mind By:

_____

_____

I Pleased My Soul By:

_____

_____

THIS WEEK I FELT

I AM LEAVING THIS WEEK FEELING...

_____

NOTES:

_____

Weekly Gratitude

Date: _____

3 things I'm grateful for this week are...

_____

_____

_____

Next week I will express my gratitude by...

_____

_____

_____

"Happiness is a habit."

Week 18

DATE _____

MY MAIN GOALS FOR THE UPCOMING WEEK ARE:

○ _____

○ _____

○ _____

It's a Bonus if I...

_____

_____

I Will Move My Body By:

_____

_____

I Will Enhance My Mind By:

_____

_____

I Will Please My Soul By:

_____

_____

REMINDER:

You have everything you need to succeed.
The magic is within you, continue to let it out and trust it.

I AM GOING INTO THIS WEEK FEELING...

_____

AFFIRM:

I define my worth and I am worthy.

Week 18 Check in

DATE _____

THIS PAST WEEK I ACHIEVED:

- ○ _____
- ○ _____
- ○ _____
- ○ _____
- ○ _____

I Moved My Body By:

_____

_____

I Enhanced My Mind By:

_____

_____

I Pleased My Soul By:

_____

_____

THIS WEEK I FELT

I AM LEAVING THIS WEEK FEELING...

_____

NOTES:

_____

Weekly Gratitude

Date: _____

3 things I'm grateful for this week are...

_____

_____

_____

Next week I will express my gratitude by...

_____

_____

_____

"Happiness is a habit."

Week 19

DATE _____

MY MAIN GOALS FOR THE UPCOMING WEEK ARE:

○ _____

○ _____

○ _____

It's a Bonus if I...

_____

_____

I Will Move My Body By:

_____

_____

I Will Enhance My Mind By:

_____

_____

I Will Please My Soul By:

_____

_____

REMINDER:

You started this journey because you know you are meant for more. You are meant to live your dream life. Don't give up now, you are so close.

I AM GOING INTO THIS WEEK FEELING...

AFFIRM:

It is my destiny to live the life of my dreams. The life of my dreams IS my reality.

Week 19 Check in

DATE _____

THIS PAST WEEK I ACHIEVED:

- ○ _____
- ○ _____
- ○ _____
- ○ _____
- ○ _____

THIS WEEK I FELT

I AM LEAVING THIS WEEK FEELING...
_____

I Moved My Body By:
_____
_____

I Enhanced My Mind By:
_____
_____

NOTES:
_____

I Pleased My Soul By:
_____
_____

Weekly Gratitude

Date: _____

3 things I'm grateful for this week are...

_____

_____

_____

Next week I will express my gratitude by...

_____

_____

_____

"Happiness is a habit."

Week 20

DATE _____

MY MAIN GOALS FOR THE UPCOMING WEEK ARE:

○ _____
○ _____
○ _____

It's a Bonus if I...

_____
_____

I Will Move My Body By:

_____
_____

I Will Enhance My Mind By:

_____
_____

I Will Please My Soul By:

_____
_____

REMINDER:

You can't help others if you aren't whole yourself. Taking care of your mind, body and soul is your priority.

I AM GOING INTO THIS WEEK FEELING...

AFFIRM:

I am precious. I am protected.

Week 20 Check in

DATE _____

THIS PAST WEEK I ACHIEVED:

- ○ _____
- ○ _____
- ○ _____
- ○ _____
- ○ _____

THIS WEEK I FELT

I AM LEAVING THIS WEEK FEELING...

I Moved My Body By:

_____

_____

I Enhanced My Mind By:

_____

_____

NOTES:

_____

I Pleased My Soul By:

_____

_____

Weekly Gratitude

Date: _____

3 things I'm grateful for this week are...

_____

_____

_____

Next week I will express my gratitude by...

_____

_____

_____

"Happiness is a habit."

DATE _____

MY MAIN GOALS FOR THE UPCOMING WEEK ARE:

○ _____
○ _____
○ _____

It's a Bonus if I...

_____
_____

I Will Move My Body By:

_____
_____

I Will Enhance My Mind By:

_____
_____

I Will Please My Soul By:

_____
_____

REMINDER:

Judgement of others is often just jealousy. You don't need to waste your time on what others think. Put the focus back on you, where it belongs.

I AM GOING INTO THIS WEEK FEELING...

AFFIRM:

I am my own powerful person, the opinion of others does not affect me.

Week 21 Check in

DATE _____

THIS PAST WEEK I ACHIEVED:

○ _____

○ _____

○ _____

○ _____

○ _____

I Moved My Body By:

_____

_____

I Enhanced My Mind By:

_____

_____

I Pleased My Soul By:

_____

_____

THIS WEEK I FELT

I AM LEAVING THIS WEEK FEELING...
_____

NOTES:
_____

Weekly Gratitude

Date: _____

3 things I'm grateful for this week are...

_____

_____

_____

Next week I will express my gratitude by...

_____

_____

_____

"Happiness is a habit."

Week 22

DATE _____

MY MAIN GOALS FOR THE UPCOMING WEEK ARE:

○ _____
○ _____
○ _____

It's a Bonus if I...

_____
_____

I Will Move My Body By:

_____
_____

I Will Enhance My Mind By:

_____
_____

I Will Please My Soul By:

_____
_____

REMINDER:

Nothing can hold you back now. Your determination and drive is admirable and it is taking you places.

I AM GOING INTO THIS WEEK FEELING...

AFFIRM:

I am unstoppable.

Week 22 Check in

DATE _____

THIS PAST WEEK I ACHIEVED:

- ○ _____
- ○ _____
- ○ _____
- ○ _____
- ○ _____

THIS WEEK I FELT

I AM LEAVING THIS WEEK FEELING...

I Moved My Body By:

_____

_____

I Enhanced My Mind By:

_____

_____

I Pleased My Soul By:

_____

_____

NOTES:

Weekly Gratitude

Date: _____

3 things I'm grateful for this week are...

_____

_____

_____

Next week I will express my gratitude by...

_____

_____

_____

"Happiness is a habit."

Week 23

DATE _____

MY MAIN GOALS FOR THE UPCOMING WEEK ARE:

○ _____
○ _____
○ _____

It's a Bonus if I...

_____
_____

I Will Move My Body By:

_____
_____

I Will Enhance My Mind By:

_____
_____

I Will Please My Soul By:

_____
_____

REMINDER:

You are in charge of your life and you control the direction of it. You hold all the power.

I AM GOING INTO THIS WEEK FEELING...

AFFIRM:

I am a good person who deserves good things.

Week 23 Check in

DATE _____

THIS PAST WEEK I ACHIEVED:

- ○ _____
- ○ _____
- ○ _____
- ○ _____
- ○ _____

THIS WEEK I FELT

I AM LEAVING THIS WEEK FEELING...
_____

I Moved My Body By:

_____

_____

I Enhanced My Mind By:

_____

_____

I Pleased My Soul By:

_____

_____

NOTES:
_____

Weekly Gratitude

Date: _____

3 things I'm grateful for this week are...

_____

_____

_____

Next week I will express my gratitude by...

_____

_____

_____

"Happiness is a habit."

Week 24

DATE _____

MY MAIN GOALS FOR THE UPCOMING WEEK ARE:

○ _____
○ _____
○ _____

It's a Bonus if I...

_____
_____

I Will Move My Body By:

_____
_____

I Will Enhance My Mind By:

_____
_____

I Will Please My Soul By:

_____
_____

REMINDER:

You have come so far already. This year is going to be life changing for you.

I AM GOING INTO THIS WEEK FEELING...

AFFIRM:

My mistakes do not define me.

Week 24 Check in

DATE _____

THIS PAST WEEK I ACHIEVED:

- ○ _____
- ○ _____
- ○ _____
- ○ _____
- ○ _____

I Moved My Body By:

_____
_____

I Enhanced My Mind By:

_____
_____

I Pleased My Soul By:

_____
_____

THIS WEEK I FELT

I AM LEAVING THIS WEEK FEELING...

_____

NOTES:

_____

Weekly Gratitude

Date: _____

3 things I'm grateful for this week are...

_____

_____

_____

Next week I will express my gratitude by...

_____

_____

_____

"Happiness is a habit."

Week 25

DATE _____

MY MAIN GOALS FOR THE UPCOMING WEEK ARE:

○ _____

○ _____

○ _____

It's a Bonus if I...

_____

_____

I Will Move My Body By:

_____

_____

I Will Enhance My Mind By:

_____

_____

I Will Please My Soul By:

_____

_____

REMINDER:

'Decide what kind of a life you want, then say NO to everything that isn't that'
~ Bob Proctor

I AM GOING INTO THIS WEEK FEELING...

AFFIRM:

I have the power to positively impact the lives of those around me.

Week 25 Check in

DATE _____

THIS PAST WEEK I ACHIEVED:

- ○ _____
- ○ _____
- ○ _____
- ○ _____
- ○ _____

THIS WEEK I FELT

I AM LEAVING THIS WEEK FEELING...
_____

I Moved My Body By:

_____

_____

I Enhanced My Mind By:

_____

_____

NOTES:

_____

I Pleased My Soul By:

_____

_____

Weekly Gratitude

Date: _____

3 things I'm grateful for this week are...

_____

_____

_____

Next week I will express my gratitude by...

_____

_____

_____

"Happiness is a habit."

Week 26

DATE _____

MY MAIN GOALS FOR THE UPCOMING WEEK ARE:

○ _____

○ _____

○ _____

REMINDER:

You are growing every week, every day, every minute. Keep going.

It's a Bonus if I...

I Will Move My Body By:

I AM GOING INTO THIS WEEK FEELING...

I Will Enhance My Mind By:

I Will Please My Soul By:

AFFIRM:

I am independent.

Week 26 Check in

DATE _____

THIS PAST WEEK I ACHIEVED:

- ○ _____
- ○ _____
- ○ _____
- ○ _____
- ○ _____

THIS WEEK I FELT

I AM LEAVING THIS WEEK FEELING...
_____

I Moved My Body By:

_____
_____

I Enhanced My Mind By:

_____
_____

I Pleased My Soul By:

_____
_____

NOTES:
_____

Weekly Gratitude

Date: _____

3 things I'm grateful for this week are...

_____

_____

_____

Next week I will express my gratitude by...

_____

_____

_____

"Happiness is a habit."

Week 27

DATE _____

MY MAIN GOALS FOR THE UPCOMING WEEK ARE:

○ _____

○ _____

○ _____

It's a Bonus if I...

_____

_____

I Will Move My Body By:

_____

_____

I Will Enhance My Mind By:

_____

_____

I Will Please My Soul By:

_____

_____

REMINDER:

You will inspire those around you with your consistency and dedication.

I AM GOING INTO THIS WEEK FEELING...

AFFIRM:

I am capable of living my dream life. I already have all I need within me.

Week 27 Check in

DATE _____

THIS PAST WEEK I ACHIEVED:

○ _____

○ _____

○ _____

○ _____

○ _____

THIS WEEK I FELT

I AM LEAVING THIS WEEK FEELING...
_____

I Moved My Body By:
_____
_____

I Enhanced My Mind By:
_____
_____

I Pleased My Soul By:
_____
_____

NOTES:
_____

Weekly Gratitude

Date: _____

3 things I'm grateful for this week are...

_____

_____

_____

Next week I will express my gratitude by...

_____

_____

_____

"Happiness is a habit."

Week 28

DATE _____

MY MAIN GOALS FOR THE UPCOMING WEEK ARE:

○ _____

○ _____

○ _____

It's a Bonus if I...

_____

_____

I Will Move My Body By:

_____

_____

I Will Enhance My Mind By:

_____

_____

I Will Please My Soul By:

_____

_____

REMINDER:

You become what you think about.. so think positively this week. Remind yourself that you are deserving of abundance.

I AM GOING INTO THIS WEEK FEELING...

AFFIRM:

I am attracting abundance effortlessly with every breath I take.

Week 28 Check in

DATE _____

THIS PAST WEEK I ACHIEVED:

- ○ _____
- ○ _____
- ○ _____
- ○ _____
- ○ _____

I Moved My Body By:

_____

_____

I Enhanced My Mind By:

_____

_____

I Pleased My Soul By:

_____

_____

THIS WEEK I FELT

I AM LEAVING THIS WEEK FEELING...

NOTES:

_____

Weekly Gratitude

Date: _____

3 things I'm grateful for this week are...

_____

_____

_____

Next week I will express my gratitude by...

_____

_____

_____

"Happiness is a habit."

DATE _____

MY MAIN GOALS FOR THE UPCOMING WEEK ARE:

○ _____

○ _____

○ _____

It's a Bonus if I...

_____

_____

I Will Move My Body By:

_____

_____

I Will Enhance My Mind By:

_____

_____

I Will Please My Soul By:

_____

_____

REMINDER:

You are more powerful than you realise. You can change your life and the life of all those around you. It all starts with you.

I AM GOING INTO THIS WEEK FEELING...

AFFIRM:

I am a cycle breaker. The positive influence I have on others knows no bounds.

Week 29 Check in

DATE _____

THIS PAST WEEK I ACHIEVED:

- ○ _____
- ○ _____
- ○ _____
- ○ _____
- ○ _____

I Moved My Body By:

_____
_____

I Enhanced My Mind By:

_____
_____

I Pleased My Soul By:

_____
_____

THIS WEEK I FELT

I AM LEAVING THIS WEEK FEELING...

_____

NOTES:

_____

Weekly Gratitude

Date: _____

3 things I'm grateful for this week are...

_____

_____

_____

Next week I will express my gratitude by...

_____

_____

_____

"Happiness is a habit."

Week 30

DATE _____

MY MAIN GOALS FOR THE UPCOMING WEEK ARE:

○ _____

○ _____

○ _____

It's a Bonus if I...

_____

_____

I Will Move My Body By:

_____

_____

I Will Enhance My Mind By:

_____

_____

I Will Please My Soul By:

_____

_____

REMINDER:

You are evolving into a more talented and experienced person each week.

I AM GOING INTO THIS WEEK FEELING...

AFFIRM:

I am an authority figure. Those around me look up to me.

Week 30 Check in

DATE _____

THIS PAST WEEK I ACHIEVED:

- ○ _____
- ○ _____
- ○ _____
- ○ _____
- ○ _____

I Moved My Body By:

_____

_____

I Enhanced My Mind By:

_____

_____

I Pleased My Soul By:

_____

_____

THIS WEEK I FELT

I AM LEAVING THIS WEEK FEELING...

_____

NOTES:

_____

Weekly Gratitude

Date: _____

3 things I'm grateful for this week are...

_____
_____
_____

Next week I will express my gratitude by...

_____
_____
_____

"Happiness is a habit."

DATE _____

MY MAIN GOALS FOR THE UPCOMING WEEK ARE:

○ _____

○ _____

○ _____

It's a Bonus if I...

_____

_____

I Will Move My Body By:

_____

_____

I Will Enhance My Mind By:

_____

_____

I Will Please My Soul By:

_____

_____

REMINDER:

You can attract anything you desire into your life, you just need to keep believing it.

I AM GOING INTO THIS WEEK FEELING...

AFFIRM:

I am aligned with my higher self.

Week 31 Check in

DATE _____

THIS PAST WEEK I ACHIEVED:

- ○ _____
- ○ _____
- ○ _____
- ○ _____
- ○ _____

I Moved My Body By:

_____

_____

I Enhanced My Mind By:

_____

_____

I Pleased My Soul By:

_____

_____

THIS WEEK I FELT

I AM LEAVING THIS WEEK FEELING...

_____

NOTES:

_____

Weekly Gratitude

Date: _____

3 things I'm grateful for this week are...

_____
_____
_____

Next week I will express my gratitude by...

_____
_____
_____

"Happiness is a habit."

Week 32

DATE _____

MY MAIN GOALS FOR THE UPCOMING WEEK ARE:

- _____
- _____
- _____

It's a Bonus if I...

_____

_____

I Will Move My Body By:

_____

_____

I Will Enhance My Mind By:

_____

_____

I Will Please My Soul By:

_____

_____

REMINDER:

You are going to expend energy regardless, don't expend it on fear and doubt, expend it on joy and hope.

I AM GOING INTO THIS WEEK FEELING...

AFFIRM:

I am emotionally mature and open.

Week 32 Check in

DATE _____

THIS PAST WEEK I ACHIEVED:

- ○ _____
- ○ _____
- ○ _____
- ○ _____
- ○ _____

THIS WEEK I FELT

I AM LEAVING THIS WEEK FEELING...

I Moved My Body By:

_____

_____

I Enhanced My Mind By:

_____

_____

NOTES:

_____

I Pleased My Soul By:

_____

_____

Weekly Gratitude

Date: _____

3 things I'm grateful for this week are...

_____

_____

_____

Next week I will express my gratitude by...

_____

_____

_____

"Happiness is a habit."

Week 33

DATE _____

MY MAIN GOALS FOR THE UPCOMING WEEK ARE:

○ _____
○ _____
○ _____

It's a Bonus if I...
_____
_____

I Will Move My Body By:
_____
_____

I Will Enhance My Mind By:
_____
_____

I Will Please My Soul By:
_____
_____

REMINDER:

Your habits are becoming a lifestyle now. Your consistency and dedication are part of your new personality. You are upgrading your life.

I AM GOING INTO THIS WEEK FEELING...
_____

AFFIRM:

I am proud of myself for not giving up.

Week 33 Check in

DATE _____

THIS PAST WEEK I ACHIEVED:

○ _____

○ _____

○ _____

○ _____

○ _____

THIS WEEK I FELT

I AM LEAVING THIS WEEK FEELING...
_____

I Moved My Body By:

_____

_____

I Enhanced My Mind By:

_____

_____

I Pleased My Soul By:

_____

_____

NOTES:
_____

Weekly Gratitude

Date: _____

3 things I'm grateful for this week are...

_____

_____

_____

Next week I will express my gratitude by...

_____

_____

_____

"Happiness is a habit."

Week 34

DATE _____

MY MAIN GOALS FOR THE UPCOMING WEEK ARE:

○ _____
○ _____
○ _____

It's a Bonus if I...
_____
_____

I Will Move My Body By:
_____
_____

I Will Enhance My Mind By:
_____
_____

I Will Please My Soul By:
_____
_____

REMINDER:

You are a combination of those you spend the most of your time with. Are the people around you reflective of the person you want to be?

I AM GOING INTO THIS WEEK FEELING...
_____

AFFIRM:

I can attract the right people into my life by staying in alignment with my best self.

Week 34 Check in

DATE _____

THIS PAST WEEK I ACHIEVED:

- ○ _____
- ○ _____
- ○ _____
- ○ _____
- ○ _____

I Moved My Body By:

_____

_____

I Enhanced My Mind By:

_____

_____

I Pleased My Soul By:

_____

_____

THIS WEEK I FELT

I AM LEAVING THIS WEEK FEELING...

_____

NOTES:

_____

Weekly Gratitude

Date: _____

3 things I'm grateful for this week are...

_____

_____

_____

Next week I will express my gratitude by...

_____

_____

_____

"Happiness is a habit."

Week 35

DATE _____

MY MAIN GOALS FOR THE UPCOMING WEEK ARE:

○ _____
○ _____
○ _____

It's a Bonus if I...

_____
_____

I Will Move My Body By:

_____
_____

I Will Enhance My Mind By:

_____
_____

I Will Please My Soul By:

_____
_____

REMINDER:

You will be able to serve people who really need it because of the abundance that is coming to you.

I AM GOING INTO THIS WEEK FEELING...

AFFIRM:

I am a healer and bring so much peace to those around me.

Week 35 Check in

DATE _____

THIS PAST WEEK I ACHIEVED:

- ○ _____
- ○ _____
- ○ _____
- ○ _____
- ○ _____

THIS WEEK I FELT

I AM LEAVING THIS WEEK FEELING...
_____

I Moved My Body By:

_____

_____

I Enhanced My Mind By:

_____

_____

NOTES:
_____

I Pleased My Soul By:

_____

_____

Weekly Gratitude

Date: _____

3 things I'm grateful for this week are...

_____

_____

_____

Next week I will express my gratitude by...

_____

_____

"Happiness is a habit."

Week 36

DATE _____

MY MAIN GOALS FOR THE UPCOMING WEEK ARE:

○ _____
○ _____
○ _____

It's a Bonus if I...
_____
_____

I Will Move My Body By:
_____
_____

I Will Enhance My Mind By:
_____
_____

I Will Please My Soul By:
_____
_____

REMINDER:

You are unique for making it this far without giving up on your goals. Most would have crumbled by now. You will be rewarded for your efforts.

I AM GOING INTO THIS WEEK FEELING...

AFFIRM:

I am a one of a kind. There is no one like me and that is my power.

Week 36 Check in

DATE _____

THIS PAST WEEK I ACHIEVED:

- ○ _____
- ○ _____
- ○ _____
- ○ _____
- ○ _____

I Moved My Body By:

_____

_____

I Enhanced My Mind By:

_____

_____

I Pleased My Soul By:

_____

_____

THIS WEEK I FELT

I AM LEAVING THIS WEEK FEELING...

NOTES:

Weekly Gratitude

Date: _____

3 things I'm grateful for this week are...

_____

_____

_____

Next week I will express my gratitude by...

_____

_____

"Happiness is a habit."

Week 37

DATE _____

MY MAIN GOALS FOR THE UPCOMING WEEK ARE:

○ _____
○ _____
○ _____

It's a Bonus if I...

_____
_____

I Will Move My Body By:

_____
_____

I Will Enhance My Mind By:

_____
_____

I Will Please My Soul By:

_____
_____

REMINDER:

You always have a choice.

I AM GOING INTO THIS WEEK FEELING...

AFFIRM:

My spirit radiates from the inside out. It warms those around me.

Week 37 Check in

DATE _____

THIS PAST WEEK I ACHIEVED:

- ○ _____
- ○ _____
- ○ _____
- ○ _____
- ○ _____

THIS WEEK I FELT

I AM LEAVING THIS WEEK FEELING...
_____

I Moved My Body By:

_____

_____

I Enhanced My Mind By:

_____

_____

I Pleased My Soul By:

_____

_____

NOTES:

_____

Weekly Gratitude

Date: _____

3 things I'm grateful for this week are...

_____

_____

_____

Next week I will express my gratitude by...

_____

_____

"Happiness is a habit."

Week 38

DATE _____

MY MAIN GOALS FOR THE UPCOMING WEEK ARE:

○ _____
○ _____
○ _____

It's a Bonus if I...

_____
_____

I Will Move My Body By:

_____
_____

I Will Enhance My Mind By:

_____
_____

I Will Please My Soul By:

_____
_____

REMINDER:

You are gifted just by having a body and a mind. You are a walking miracle who can have whatever you want.

I AM GOING INTO THIS WEEK FEELING...

AFFIRM:

I am deserving of great love and finances.

Week 38 Check in

DATE _____

THIS PAST WEEK I ACHIEVED:

- ○ _____
- ○ _____
- ○ _____
- ○ _____
- ○ _____

I Moved My Body By:

_____
_____

I Enhanced My Mind By:

_____
_____

I Pleased My Soul By:

_____
_____

THIS WEEK I FELT

I AM LEAVING THIS WEEK FEELING...

NOTES:

_____

Weekly Gratitude

Date: _____

3 things I'm grateful for this week are...

_____

_____

_____

Next week I will express my gratitude by...

_____

_____

"Happiness is a habit."

DATE _____

MY MAIN GOALS FOR THE UPCOMING WEEK ARE:

○ _____
○ _____
○ _____

It's a Bonus if I...

_____
_____

I Will Move My Body By:

_____
_____

I Will Enhance My Mind By:

_____
_____

I Will Please My Soul By:

_____
_____

REMINDER:

Your life and work has meaning. You have the power to inspire those around you.

I AM GOING INTO THIS WEEK FEELING...

AFFIRM:

I am receptive to all the good in the universe.

Week 39 Check in

DATE _____

THIS PAST WEEK I ACHIEVED:

- ○ _____
- ○ _____
- ○ _____
- ○ _____
- ○ _____

I Moved My Body By:

_____

_____

I Enhanced My Mind By:

_____

_____

I Pleased My Soul By:

_____

_____

THIS WEEK I FELT

I AM LEAVING THIS WEEK FEELING...

_____

NOTES:

_____

Weekly Gratitude

Date: _____

3 things I'm grateful for this week are...

_____

_____

_____

Next week I will express my gratitude by...

_____

_____

"Happiness is a habit."

Week 40

DATE _____

MY MAIN GOALS FOR THE UPCOMING WEEK ARE:

○ _____

○ _____

○ _____

It's a Bonus if I...

_____

_____

I Will Move My Body By:

_____

_____

I Will Enhance My Mind By:

_____

_____

I Will Please My Soul By:

_____

_____

REMINDER:

You are appreciated.

I AM GOING INTO THIS WEEK FEELING...

AFFIRM:

I am wanted and admired.

Week 40 Check in

DATE _____

THIS PAST WEEK I ACHIEVED:

- ○ _____
- ○ _____
- ○ _____
- ○ _____
- ○ _____

THIS WEEK I FELT

I AM LEAVING THIS WEEK FEELING...

I Moved My Body By:

_____
_____

I Enhanced My Mind By:

_____
_____

NOTES:
_____

I Pleased My Soul By:

_____
_____

Weekly Gratitude

Date: _____

3 things I'm grateful for this week are...

_____

_____

_____

Next week I will express my gratitude by...

_____

_____

"Happiness is a habit."

Week 41

DATE _____

MY MAIN GOALS FOR THE UPCOMING WEEK ARE:

○ _____
○ _____
○ _____

It's a Bonus if I...

_____
_____

I Will Move My Body By:

_____
_____

I Will Enhance My Mind By:

_____
_____

I Will Please My Soul By:

_____
_____

REMINDER:
_____

You have made such amazing progress in the past few months. Don't give up when you're close to the next level of success.

I AM GOING INTO THIS WEEK FEELING...
_____

AFFIRM:
_____
I am a magnet to money.

Week 41 Check in

DATE _____

THIS PAST WEEK I ACHIEVED:

- ○ _____
- ○ _____
- ○ _____
- ○ _____
- ○ _____

THIS WEEK I FELT

I AM LEAVING THIS WEEK FEELING...
_____

I Moved My Body By:

_____
_____

I Enhanced My Mind By:

_____
_____

NOTES:
_____

I Pleased My Soul By:

_____
_____

Weekly Gratitude

Date: _____

3 things I'm grateful for this week are...

_____

_____

_____

Next week I will express my gratitude by...

_____

_____

"Happiness is a habit."

Week 42

DATE _____

MY MAIN GOALS FOR THE UPCOMING WEEK ARE:

○ _____
○ _____
○ _____

It's a Bonus if I...

_____
_____

I Will Move My Body By:

_____
_____

I Will Enhance My Mind By:

_____
_____

I Will Please My Soul By:

_____
_____

REMINDER:

You have skills and talent that you haven't even discovered yet. There is no limit to your abilities. The longer you stay consistent, the more you will discover.

I AM GOING INTO THIS WEEK FEELING...
_____

AFFIRM:

I have a good heart and that will bring real love and the right people to me.

Week 42 Check in

DATE _____

THIS PAST WEEK I ACHIEVED:

- ○ _____
- ○ _____
- ○ _____
- ○ _____
- ○ _____

THIS WEEK I FELT

I AM LEAVING THIS WEEK FEELING...
_____

I Moved My Body By:

_____
_____

I Enhanced My Mind By:

_____
_____

NOTES:
_____

I Pleased My Soul By:

_____
_____

Weekly Gratitude

Date: _____

3 things I'm grateful for this week are...

_____

_____

_____

Next week I will express my gratitude by...

_____

_____

"Happiness is a habit."

DATE _____

MY MAIN GOALS FOR THE UPCOMING WEEK ARE:

○ _____
○ _____
○ _____

It's a Bonus if I...

_____
_____

I Will Move My Body By:

_____
_____

I Will Enhance My Mind By:

_____
_____

I Will Please My Soul By:

_____
_____

REMINDER:

It is never too late to make a real difference in your life. Small actions can have a huge impact.

I AM GOING INTO THIS WEEK FEELING...

AFFIRM:

I stick to my word and can trust myself deeply.

Week 43 Check in

DATE _____

THIS PAST WEEK I ACHIEVED:

○ _____

○ _____

○ _____

○ _____

○ _____

THIS WEEK I FELT

I AM LEAVING THIS WEEK FEELING...
_____

I Moved My Body By:

_____

_____

I Enhanced My Mind By:

_____

_____

NOTES:
_____

I Pleased My Soul By:

_____

_____

Weekly Gratitude

Date: _____

3 things I'm grateful for this week are...

_____

_____

_____

Next week I will express my gratitude by...

_____

_____

"Happiness is a habit."

DATE _____

MY MAIN GOALS FOR THE UPCOMING WEEK ARE:

○ _____
○ _____
○ _____

It's a Bonus if I...
_____
_____

I Will Move My Body By:
_____
_____

I Will Enhance My Mind By:
_____
_____

I Will Please My Soul By:
_____
_____

REMINDER:
_____

You don't need to wait for others to live the life you are dreaming of. You can give it all to yourself.

I AM GOING INTO THIS WEEK FEELING...
_____

AFFIRM:
_____
I am in awe of myself.

Week 44 Check in

DATE _____

THIS PAST WEEK I ACHIEVED:

- ○ _____
- ○ _____
- ○ _____
- ○ _____
- ○ _____

THIS WEEK I FELT

I AM LEAVING THIS WEEK FEELING...
_____

I Moved My Body By:
_____
_____

I Enhanced My Mind By:
_____
_____

I Pleased My Soul By:
_____
_____

NOTES:
_____

Weekly Gratitude

Date: _____

3 things I'm grateful for this week are...

_____
_____
_____

Next week I will express my gratitude by...

_____
_____

"Happiness is a habit."

Week 45

DATE _____

MY MAIN GOALS FOR THE UPCOMING WEEK ARE:

○ _____
○ _____
○ _____

It's a Bonus if I...

_____
_____

I Will Move My Body By:

_____
_____

I Will Enhance My Mind By:

_____
_____

I Will Please My Soul By:

_____
_____

REMINDER:

You have stayed consistent for so long, you are capable of continuing this consistency and manifesting all you've ever dreamed of.

I AM GOING INTO THIS WEEK FEELING...

_____

AFFIRM:

I am healing every day. I have the power to continue healing myself.

Week 45 Check in

DATE _____

THIS PAST WEEK I ACHIEVED:

- ○ _____
- ○ _____
- ○ _____
- ○ _____
- ○ _____

I Moved My Body By:

_____
_____

I Enhanced My Mind By:

_____
_____

I Pleased My Soul By:

_____
_____

THIS WEEK I FELT

I AM LEAVING THIS WEEK FEELING...

_____

NOTES:

_____

Weekly Gratitude

Date: _____

3 things I'm grateful for this week are...

_____

_____

_____

Next week I will express my gratitude by...

_____

_____

"Happiness is a habit."

Week 46

DATE _____

MY MAIN GOALS FOR THE UPCOMING WEEK ARE:

- ○ _____
- ○ _____
- ○ _____

It's a Bonus if I...

_____
_____

I Will Move My Body By:

_____
_____

I Will Enhance My Mind By:

_____
_____

I Will Please My Soul By:

_____
_____

REMINDER:

You are making so much progress. You should feel incredibly proud.

I AM GOING INTO THIS WEEK FEELING...

AFFIRM:

I provide peace to those around me just by being me.

Week 46 Check in

DATE _____

THIS PAST WEEK I ACHIEVED:

- ○ _____
- ○ _____
- ○ _____
- ○ _____
- ○ _____

I Moved My Body By:

_____

_____

I Enhanced My Mind By:

_____

_____

I Pleased My Soul By:

_____

_____

THIS WEEK I FELT

I AM LEAVING THIS WEEK FEELING...

_____

NOTES:

_____

Weekly Gratitude

Date: _____

3 things I'm grateful for this week are...

_____

_____

_____

Next week I will express my gratitude by...

_____

_____

"Happiness is a habit."

Week 47

DATE _____

MY MAIN GOALS FOR THE UPCOMING WEEK ARE:

○ _____
○ _____
○ _____

It's a Bonus if I...

_____
_____

I Will Move My Body By:

_____
_____

I Will Enhance My Mind By:

_____
_____

I Will Please My Soul By:

_____
_____

REMINDER:

Every week you are getting closer to your dream life, to all you've ever desired. You are so close now.

I AM GOING INTO THIS WEEK FEELING...

AFFIRM:

I am the creator of my reality and I can manifest anything I want.

Week 47 Check in

DATE _____

THIS PAST WEEK I ACHIEVED:

- ○ _____
- ○ _____
- ○ _____
- ○ _____
- ○ _____

THIS WEEK I FELT

I AM LEAVING THIS WEEK FEELING...
_____

I Moved My Body By:

_____

_____

I Enhanced My Mind By:

_____

_____

NOTES:
_____

I Pleased My Soul By:

_____

_____

Weekly Gratitude

Date: _____

3 things I'm grateful for this week are...

_____
_____
_____

Next week I will express my gratitude by...

_____
_____

"Happiness is a habit."

Week 48

DATE _____

MY MAIN GOALS FOR THE UPCOMING WEEK ARE:

○ _____

○ _____

○ _____

It's a Bonus if I...

_____

_____

I Will Move My Body By:

_____

_____

I Will Enhance My Mind By:

_____

_____

I Will Please My Soul By:

_____

_____

REMINDER:

YOU have got yourself to where you are right now. You can take all the credit for the abundance in your life - you deeply deserve it.

I AM GOING INTO THIS WEEK FEELING...

_____

AFFIRM:

I am so proud of myself for overcoming all of the hurdles I have ever faced.

Week 48 Check in

DATE _____

THIS PAST WEEK I ACHIEVED:

- ○ _____
- ○ _____
- ○ _____
- ○ _____
- ○ _____

THIS WEEK I FELT

I AM LEAVING THIS WEEK FEELING...

I Moved My Body By:

_____
_____

I Enhanced My Mind By:

_____
_____

NOTES:

I Pleased My Soul By:

_____
_____

Weekly Gratitude

Date: _____

3 things I'm grateful for this week are...

_____

_____

_____

Next week I will express my gratitude by...

_____

_____

"Happiness is a habit."

Week 49

DATE: _____

MY MAIN GOALS FOR THE UPCOMING WEEK ARE:

- ○ _____
- ○ _____
- ○ _____

It's a Bonus if I...

_____
_____

I Will Move My Body By:

_____
_____

I Will Enhance My Mind By:

_____
_____

I Will Please My Soul By:

_____
_____

REMINDER:

You are proving that limitless transformation is possible. You are an inspiration.

I AM GOING INTO THIS WEEK FEELING...

_____

AFFIRM:

I am focused and nothing can stop me.

Week 49 Check in

DATE _____

THIS PAST WEEK I ACHIEVED:

○ _____

○ _____

○ _____

○ _____

○ _____

THIS WEEK I FELT

I AM LEAVING THIS WEEK FEELING... _____

I Moved My Body By:

_____

_____

I Enhanced My Mind By:

_____

_____

I Pleased My Soul By:

_____

_____

NOTES:

_____

Weekly Gratitude

Date: _____

3 things I'm grateful for this week are...

_____

_____

_____

Next week I will express my gratitude by...

_____

_____

"Happiness is a habit."

DATE_____

MY MAIN GOALS FOR THE UPCOMING WEEK ARE:

○ _____
○ _____
○ _____

It's a Bonus if I...
_____
_____

I Will Move My Body By:
_____
_____

I Will Enhance My Mind By:
_____
_____

I Will Please My Soul By:
_____
_____

REMINDER:

Your dreams and desires are why you started working on yourself, don't stop until you've reached your ideal destination.

I AM GOING INTO THIS WEEK FEELING...

AFFIRM:

I can rise above any negative energy that comes towards me.

Week 50 Check in

DATE _____

THIS PAST WEEK I ACHIEVED:

- ○ _____
- ○ _____
- ○ _____
- ○ _____
- ○ _____

THIS WEEK I FELT

I AM LEAVING THIS WEEK FEELING...
_____

I Moved My Body By:

_____

_____

I Enhanced My Mind By:

_____

_____

I Pleased My Soul By:

_____

_____

NOTES:
_____

Weekly Gratitude

Date: _____

3 things I'm grateful for this week are...

_____
_____
_____

Next week I will express my gratitude by...

_____
_____

"Happiness is a habit."

Week 51

DATE _____

MY MAIN GOALS FOR THE UPCOMING WEEK ARE:

○ _____
○ _____
○ _____

It's a Bonus if I...

_____
_____

I Will Move My Body By:

_____
_____

I Will Enhance My Mind By:

_____
_____

I Will Please My Soul By:

_____
_____

REMINDER:

You are a living example of determination and a refusal to quit.

You are inspiring.

I AM GOING INTO THIS WEEK FEELING...

_____

AFFIRM:

I am being rewarded now. Abundance is showing up in all areas of my life.

Week 51 Check in

DATE _____

THIS PAST WEEK I ACHIEVED:

- ○ _____
- ○ _____
- ○ _____
- ○ _____
- ○ _____

I Moved My Body By:

_____

_____

I Enhanced My Mind By:

_____

_____

I Pleased My Soul By:

_____

_____

THIS WEEK I FELT

I AM LEAVING THIS WEEK FEELING...

_____

NOTES:

_____

Weekly Gratitude

Date: _____

3 things I'm grateful for this week are...

_____
_____
_____

Next week I will express my gratitude by...

_____
_____

"Happiness is a habit."

Week 52

DATE _____

MY MAIN GOALS FOR THE UPCOMING WEEK ARE:

○ _____
○ _____
○ _____

It's a Bonus if I...
_____
_____

I Will Move My Body By:
_____
_____

I Will Enhance My Mind By:
_____
_____

I Will Please My Soul By:
_____
_____

REMINDER:

There is no limit to the levels of success you can experience. And you deserve it all.

I AM GOING INTO THIS WEEK FEELING...
_____

AFFIRM:

I am successful, I am beautiful, I am powerful, I am unstoppable.

Week 52 Check in

DATE _____

THIS PAST WEEK I ACHIEVED:

- ○ _____
- ○ _____
- ○ _____
- ○ _____
- ○ _____

THIS WEEK I FELT

I AM LEAVING THIS WEEK FEELING...

I Moved My Body By:

_____
_____

I Enhanced My Mind By:

_____
_____

I Pleased My Soul By:

_____
_____

NOTES:

_____

Weekly Gratitude

Date: _____

3 things I'm grateful for this week are...

_____

_____

_____

Next week I will express my gratitude by...

_____

_____

"Happiness is a habit."

Congratulations!

You have just completed 52 weeks of goal setting and reflection, you must feel so aligned and proud.

The next few pages have been created for you to journal on your experiences.

How has this journey made you feel?
What skills have you learned along the way?
What changes have taken place in your life?
How different does your life look now?

There is no structure to this reflection process, just let your emotions and thoughts out onto the paper as you close off this part of your journey.

JOIN US!

We have a community of beautiful humans all discovering their inner magic and improving their lives on Instagram!

On our page you'll find lots of motivational and spiritual content and we'd love to have you as a part of our family!
Find us at:

@TheMagicWithin_

Copyright © 2022 by TheMagicWithin. All rights reserved.
No part of this publication may be reproduced, stored or transmitted in any form or by any means, electronic, mechanical, photocopying, recording, scanning, or otherwise without written permission from the publisher.
It is illegal to copy this book, post it to a website, or distribute it by any other means without permission.

www.ingramcontent.com/pod-product-compliance
Lightning Source LLC
Chambersburg PA
CBHW081617100526
44590CB00021B/3484